White Light

An Inspiring Craft Devotional for you to SHINE in a
purpose filled life

Amber Ernst

Coming from a long line of crafty women who crochet, quilt, mend, paint, and assemble, you could say creating is in my blood (or more likely my hands). These women use(d) their gifts to bring beauty to the world and connect through craft.

For Agatha, Gladys, Joyce, Karen, and Claudia who continue to inspire. Your gifts shine so bright and I'm glad to bask in that light and hopefully reflect a little back.

TABLE OF CONTENTS

Introduction   iv

I Am Known   1

I Am Content   7

I Am Loved   13

I Am Not Alone   19

I Am Joyful   25

I Am Grateful   31

I Am Worthy   37

I Am Strong   43

I Am Calm   49

I Am Helpful   55

I Am Merry   61

I Am Kind   67

I Am Forgiven   73

I Am Unifying   79

TABLE OF CONTENTS

I Am Observant   85

I Am Traditional   91

I Am Restful   97

I Am Lighthearted   103

I Am Persevering   109

I Am Creative   115

I Am Hopeful   121

I Am Positive   127

I Am Present   133

I Am Curious   139

I Am Purposeful   145

Templates   152

About Author   162

Acknowledgments   163

References   164

Introduction

How can I use my gifts to shine?

How can they help fulfill my purpose?

Anyone who knows me knows rainbow is my favorite accent color – the brighter, the better. The unexpected happiness and sheer joy brought by all the colors together are really unmatched. If we think of each our gifts as a color, together we bring a rainbow to the world we live in. *White light* can be defined as, "apparently colorless light, which contains all the wavelengths of the visible spectrum at equal intensity." A hidden rainbow, if you will. We don't see a person's individual gifts/colors with our eyes but when they blend together, we see them *shine*. The light, our gifts, show a path for others.

This book acts as a prism, parsing out each color and looking at how that gift can guide your purpose. In each chapter we'll walk through a brief story, prayer, discussion and inspiration. Some chapters might resonate more than others because each of our stories is unique. You'll find craft inspiration but not full tutorials. Tangible crafts often reflect abstract truths, and exploring them can help you enhance or connect to your purpose.

I set out to write this book that I would have reached for, as I longed to truly fit in an organized religion and discover my place (a very colorful bold place). It was written as a series of reminders to myself, and it's meant to be kept to open up for a new idea, note, or to share with a friend.

We're going to learn about what God has laid out for our lives, and along the way we'll uncover ideas to leverage our gifts. You have so much to offer! With God's plan and our gifts, our lives have peace. We gain the contentment that comes with knowing we're on the correct path- a bumpy, windy, doesn't ever feel too straight path-and we are *not* alone.

Let's walk together – I can already see how you SHINE!

P.S. As we're all on a journey, we're walking together. We learn and polish each other. Use #mywhitelight to share any "a-ha" moments, thoughts, crafts, or ideas!

you are
KNOWN

Chapter One

I Am Known

White light seems colorless. Sometimes the hardest person to see clearly is yourself. Taking the plank out of my own eye first. Between body image, self-confidence, self-awareness, and self-talk, I am by far my own worst critic, and I know many readers can relate. If you asked me five years ago if I shine, I probably would have said, "No!" and even laughed. After all, I didn't want to stand out, to seem too big or dramatic, or stray from what was traditionally acceptable. In my mind, a quiet housewife seemed to meet societal norms the best.

One of my sister-in-laws recently told me, "You don't really let your guard down or show your true self until you know someone really well." She meant it as a casual observation, but it felt like my face had just been splashed with cold water. *What? I do that? Is it intentional? Am I afraid of what a new person would think or say about me?* I think things like: *Should I hide my tattoos when we meet? Is my technicolor fanny "too much"? What might we have in common that would be good conversation topics?*

I do have a close group of family and friends that know me. The deeper, more authentic, more of who I am daily me. I also have work colleagues, acquaintances, and friends from school long ago who know a different version of me, as we only spend limited time together. You probably have similar spheres of people in your life.

Our lives change and grow. Our personalities, knowledge, and life experiences are constantly shaping us—changing even what "me" looks like to ourselves. It feels a little unstable, learning new information about yourself. After all, I should be the one that knows myself best, right? I've realized that that assumption can sometimes be pretty far off. Sometimes the thing you've been trying to hide or you were embarrassed about is already known or more obvious than you think. God knows us.

"You have searched me, Lord, and you know me. Before a word is on my tongue you, Lord, know it completely." (Psalm 139:1, 4)

God knows us more deeply than we can imagine. He knows the wants and desires of our hearts and sees what we choose to portray to others. He sees the inside, all our brilliant colors, and how we shine in our actions toward others.

Being known doesn't equate to always being liked, fitting in, or having an easy life but we can **find peace** in knowing that even as we're discovering more about ourselves each day, we are known—truly and incomprehensibly known. I don't have to struggle with my identity or worry as it changes—You know me, and I am not alone.

God, help me to show myself as you see me.

It can feel hard to let others see a true version of me. Even made in your image, I want to hide all my inadequacies and flaws. **Do not let me be afraid or cover my light, hiding the beautiful gifts you gave me.**

Lead others to you through me and my actions.

Help me to see others as you know them - seeing, appreciating and speaking about their gifts.

AMEN.

Where is one area of my life that I hide? How can I turn it into something positive?

What is something you notice, know, or admire about a close friend or family member? Text or send a card to let them know.

How can we be more gentle with ourself and others knowing we are all growing and changing?

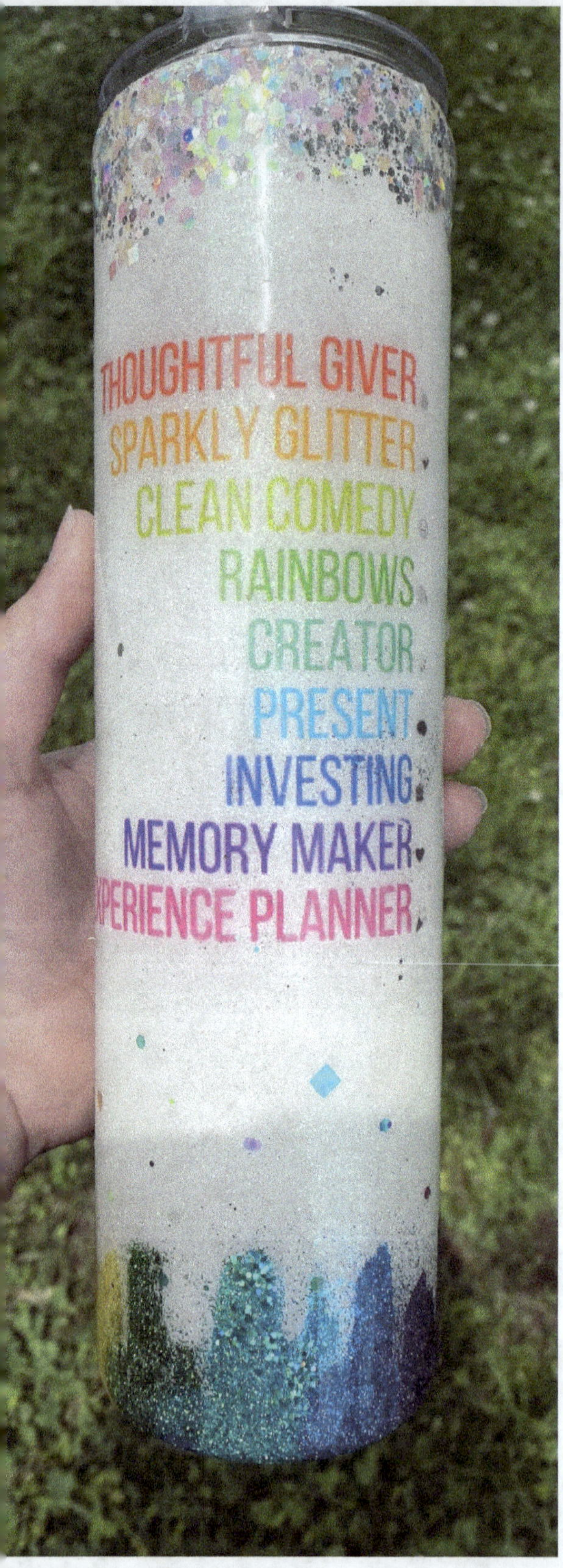

THOUGHTFUL GIVER
SPARKLY GLITTER
CLEAN COMEDY
RAINBOWS
CREATOR
PRESENT
INVESTING
MEMORY MAKER
EXPERIENCE PLANNER

If you had a cup listing *things you love,* **parts of your identify,** *what you are striving for ....how* would you be known?!

List some here

What do you want to be known for?

you are
CONTENT

Chapter Two

I Am Content

I still ask myself, *What do you want to be when you grow up?* It feels like I'm just not in the right spot. When will I feel content and stop the search for more?

From my youthful dreams (dolphin trainer or neuroscientist) to now my office and training work, there's a constant nagging feeling that I'm not enough, that I'm not doing enough. And that's just the work component; I also need to be the best wife, mother, friend, aunt, sister, and the list goes on. Even writing that makes me feel anxious, but that's how our brains work. How can I do it all? Is there a balance?

If I just push *this* much harder, organize and plan even more I can stay on top, right? What a wearying life to lead.

A quote that's stayed with me ever since I read it is:

> "I worked hard for everything I ever cared about, and nothing I ever cared about cost a single cent." (Hepworth 2019)

Let that sink in. Maybe read it again. What do you care about most? What does all your "work" get you?

The "work" in my life almost always leads away. It is so incredibly easy to go through the daily motions of life and not pause, not consider that which I'm working for. I just work. That's what we all do, right?

For so long, achievement has been the goal—in our personal and professional lives. Get the promotion, the new job; get married, have kids. Always focused on the next step. Daily just *buried* in what needs to get done to make it happen.

Achieving and planning are future focused. Not wishing away the present, but not living in it either.

God gives us this message:

> "His divine power has given us everything we need for a godly life." (2 Peter 1:3)

We have it. God gives us all we need. There is no work or achievement that will bring us anything "more." As humans we'll struggle daily but the to-do list doesn't disappear. Intentional focus on His plan and purpose for my life takes the weight off my shoulders.

When I feel the *want* of the next step or "more things" creeping in, I know I can rest in the knowledge that I have all I need. I can **take an inward focus** when the rest of the world pushes for more.

God, quiet my heart when seeking more. Show me that I am enough and what I seek won't bring me closer to You.

Let me focus and listen on what is truly important when you already provide all I need.

Help me shift my focus off worldly achievement and desires so that others see you too.

AMEN.

What is the next achievement I'm working toward? Is it in God's plan for me?

I might have everything I need but I can also be God's hands and provide for the needs of others. What can I donate, purchase, or give to another who is in need close to home or far away?

*sometimes the gift of time and knowledge are ways you can give

Read 2 Corinthians 9:8. How does God providing all you need and good works coincide?

We have all we need and sometimes a new way to shift our perspective is to change the placement.

That's why rearranging can have us feeling so good.

Do you have an office space that just needs a refresh- I love pegboards for fun supply organization....and obviously lots of color.

Maybe an unused closet can become a reading nook complete with secret book shelf? !

Where in your house, could you look *with fresh eyes* and create a place that serves those who live there using pieces you already have?

When you realize nothing is lacking, the whole world belongs to you.

LAO TZU

you are

LOVED

Chapter Three

I Am Loved

Love is simple, right? Treat people with kindness. But loving others can be way easier than loving myself. If you ask me to love myself or even see myself the way God does — after all, we're made in his image — I tear up. How? How can he love *me with all of my mistakes*?

My defenses are sky high when it comes to reflecting on my behavior, my action, my sin. I read the Word. I understand the meaning but I harden my heart and refuse to let it sink in.

We see the shepherd chasing the stray lamb. We see the welcome of the prodigal son. There are many biblical examples of His love and one that struck me was the film *Redeeming Love* based on Hosea and Gomer. Hosea is called to love the prostitute, Gomer, again and again after she strays from him. This version struck me as it was marriage focused and at the core is a lasting commitment. The betrayal felt more cruel, more cutting, more heart-breaking. I realized our relationship with God is even closer. *How could he love like that? How can God love like that? How can I love like that?*

Those tough questions push for answers, examples, and my eyes to look toward and forward to models of His love.

It's the selflessness, the unconditional part that escapes my logical mind. It's tough to admit, but it feels easier to love when someone is kind, or does what you want, or you get something out of it.

We're called to love all our neighbors—not just the ones we like. We're called to love people who don't earn it, who don't treat us how we think they should. Ephesians 2:4 says,

"But God is rich in mercy because of His great love for us...it is by grace you have been saved."

His love is unconditional. There is nothing I can do to earn or "unearn" this pure love.

While still a seemingly simple conclusion, this one hits home the hardest. It's hard to read without a lump in my throat. I still feel immensely unworthy, and modeling that love for others seems like an impossible task.

Love comes from the inside out. Maybe you're like me and struggle to see it in yourself and let it shine. The best news is that it's still there, quietly waiting to be embraced, known, and shared and that truly does make me feel loved.

God, let me feel your love **without** reserve, **without** unworthiness creeping in, without guilt over my past.

Help me feel your whole awe-inspiring love everyday.

Little by little, seeing how you love me, I can be a light and model Your example of love to others.

AMEN.

What is one way you show love to yourself?*

_____

_____

_____

What can you remind yourself when someone feels
hard to love?

_____

_____

_____

Where do you see examples of truly unconditional
love in your life? How do you know?

_____

_____

_____

Watercolor can be one of the least intimidating art forms.

The free flowing nature lends itself to a true escape.

Following simple shapes even creates beautiful cards and pictures. I love *Youtube tutorials* (see recommendation list for my favorites) for an absolute easy place to get started.

Nature (and animals) are a great place to feel love connected to an abundance of space and freedom.

These make a great date night or friend activity!

What is something you could paint, draw, or color to show love to yourself or another?

Not anything in all of creation, will be able to separate us from the love of god.

ROMANS 8:38

you are
NOT
ALONE

Chapter Four

I Am Not Alone

Facing something new can be scary. Whether it's a new job, navigating being a new parent, or handling a diagnosis, we're constantly faced with challenges and changes in our daily lives.

On my most recent birthday trip, we embarked on one of those aerial ropes courses. All colorful ropes with multiple levels where you have a harness and a clip tethering you to the route. From afar, it seemed like fun – the colors, the smiles, the laughs. Until we were stepping out on the first obstacle, and then the fear set in.

It's a long way down. Am I sure this is clipped in well? Am I brave enough to do this? So many thoughts raced through my mind.

For the first half of the time we were there I stayed on "easier" obstacles, ones that I could maneuver with little risk—until my son got stuck further out. The only way there was across some tiny pedestals with not even a support rail. Mama bear instinct kicked in, and I decided I was getting to him no matter what it took. I stepped first and kept momentum, only to miss a step. But I didn't come crashing down. I was held up by the tether and kept going. Connected to the course, I was in place right where I needed to be and so I was caught as I fell.

When I reached my son, we began navigating further and higher together, which became much easier with fear out of the way. If only I had realized from the beginning, it was never about how much I could do but the unwavering support that held me up.

Later my son was frozen in fear at another obstacle and said, "I believe in myself. You always tell me that, mom." A woman overheard and noted, "You're a good mom." I didn't quite know what to say; we rarely get mom compliments "in the wild." Looking back, I see it in a slightly different light.

If I wasn't able to set an example myself, taking that first step and misstep, my son might not have seen what he could do. We would have stopped our adventure much earlier, not even realizing all the excitement we would have missed. In Hebrews 13:5 we read,

"Never will I leave you; never will I forsake you."

Life can feel scary when we think we're walking alone. When we learn to rely on God and see how he truly "has our back," the path is much easier. We feel more confident to conquer more and can be an example to others – to family, to strangers (even on ropes courses), and to friends.

God is **ever present**. We may not feel the rope tethering us until we need it most, but it's always there and available to tug on at any time.

God, thank you for keeping us close to you everyday - anchored in Your love.

Help me feel your presence at all times. When I'm out in the world and even in quiet places.

Knowing I am not alone provides comfort and strength in my journey. Let me show that to everyone I meet.

AMEN.

Write a reminder for yourself when something is new, hard or a big change.

_____

_____

_____

_____

Where do you go when you feel alone - for quiet reflection? to immerse in a group of friends? into nature?

_____

_____

_____

_____

How do you best support when someone you know it going through a new life stage or change?

_____

_____

_____

_____

One way to show others we are not alone and to connect is through words. Sending or making cards is an easy way to show up in any life circumstances - good, bad, or my favorite, just because.

Printing on a laser printer you can run through a laminator with foil sheets to create colorful reflective cards that feel fun and unique.

Find this card and two more in the Templates section

The Lord himself goes before you and will be with you

DEUTERONOMY 31:8

you are
JOYFUL

Chapter Five

I am Joyful

The sploosh of Power Rangers diving in mud as your son plays on a perfect 75 degree day.

The slow sunrise in a foreign city as you watch the valley below fill up inch by inch with light.

The comradery and companionship as you learn an empowering veil dance for the first time.

The epic kitchen family dance to "St. Elmo's Fire" while using utensils to pound the rhythm on any nearby surface.

The surprise of a colorful rainbow bike display against a lush green tree lined street on a morning commute.

I love finding **happiness in the little moments**. The in between. The quick feeling of contentment, that all is right in the world, washing over before time marches on.

For the longest time, I confused happiness and love. I would say I *love* glitter, but really, it brings me a burst of happiness, an instant mood lift. I don't have a deep connection or affection for it. Glitter makes my heart happy would be more accurate. In our casual English language, you hear "I love that" or other variations frequently but never "That brings me joy" or "I delight in that."

Language is powerful, and love is a strong word. Happiness seems to have an effervescent quality—fleeting and leaving quickly—but it's no less impactful.

Psalm 30:5 infamously notes,

"Weeping   may   stay   for the night,   but rejoicing comes in the morning."

When we're going through times of sorrow or grief it can be comforting to note that everything is temporary and "joy comes in the morning." We rarely move through a major life incident quickly; most often the emotions and feelings linger. Joy and gratitude are an intertwined rope that pulls us along in our lives. Every day, each of those moments are a little tug pulling you through difficult times. "Building up our joy muscles" everyday keeps us strong to help others do the same.

In her book Joyful, Ingrid Fetell Lee notes that joy isn't just the icing on the cake; it's part of the cake. Discounting joy or dismissing it as non-essential negates the true reason we experience it.

Spotting happiness, noticing what activities, people, and objects delight you, puts your heart in a grateful place. Look at what surrounds you! From the smallest moment of catching a smile, to watching the stars, to the feel of a hand in yours, the connected joy and gratitude keeps you grounded.

God is our true joy. After all, joy is one of the fruits of the Spirit. He is the ultimate creator, and our joy is in Him. We are filled with joy in His presence, as we take time to notice the little, barely perceptible occasions happening around us constantly.

God, your joy surrounds me. Help me feel the joyful moments every day.

Your joy always abounds. Help me show confidence in joy, and using this gift daily.

Use my joyful heart to inspire others. **I want to show others that true joy is in You.**

AMEN.

Write your own definitions for love and joy. How difficult was this for you?

_____

_____

_____

_____

What is an easy adjustment to my routine to "flex my joy muscles"?

_____

_____

_____

_____

How can understanding joy help us in our future? What was God's design for this gift?

_____

_____

_____

_____

Joy radiates. It bursts forth lighting up smiles and filling our chest with what feels like bubbles of happiness, knowing who our Savior is.

- Create your own happy work of art - list all things, people, places, smells, tastes....anything that brings you joy
- Make a calendar and fit in 10 minutes a day or even starting with a week of just activities that bring contentment or happiness.
- Carve out time for joyful people in your life - let them know how much you love to be around them

you are
GRATEFUL

Chapter Six

I Am Grateful

I watched my purse get stolen once. You're probably thinking, *That sure is a weird way to begin this chapter,* and you're not wrong. *Did she say she watched it get stolen?* And yes...that's how it happened.

I was meeting my sister-in-law at the park to chat and watch our kids play. I arrived early and took my keys and phone with me to the playground just a short distance away—still in sight of my vehicle. As I sat on the bench, I noticed a car next to mine even though the parking lot was fairly empty. I'm an overly paranoid person and thought many times about going over, just walking closer to look, but a car next to mine is no reason to be alarmed, right?

I noticed someone exit the other vehicle, and when they came back they took awhile to get back inside—but then they sped away out of the parking lot. I thought that was weird, so I went to go check, and sure enough he or she made off and had already tried making purchases. I was still a little shaken, and I was beating myself up for not checking, not just bringing my purse (even though I could see my van), not just pushing the lock button on the keys in my hands to warn a burglar. But I realized nothing of any value was gone.

My kids were safe. I had my keys. I had enough gas to get home. I was going to be ok. Yes, I could have handled things differently in a million ways, but there was no correcting the past.

What made all the difference was the after. Explaining to my two young sons why I was scared but also, why we were ok—that they hadn't taken anything I loved, anything that couldn't be replaced. And holding them oh so close.

The minutes felt fast, rushing to get cards shut off, calling the bank, but the time after was slow. Soaking in how that fleeting moment flew by, but cast everything else after in a crystal-clear lens. A looking glass so bright it almost hurt to take it all in.

I was going to be ok. I had everything that mattered. I didn't "lose" anything; I **gained clarity,** and for that I'm grateful.

Just like happiness—gratitude mostly feels like easy, happy, memorable moments. Ones saved for "I'm grateful for..." lists or mantras. But gratefulness can also be for the tough experiences or times. The reward may only be visible on the inside, a hardened badge of honor we carry with us.

1 Thessalonians 5:18 says,

> "Give thanks in all circumstances; for this is God's will
> for you in Christ Jesus."

The word *all* gets me there. Not in some circumstances, or just the ones where it's easy but all.

Reading this page may be one thing, but the world is a dark, scary place and we have incredibly despairing events we see or experience over the course of a lifetime. We are not to make light of these events but realize an obstacle can transform into an opportunity through a lens of gratitude.

God, thanking you is easy when my life is going well. Help me to feel **grateful in all circumstances.**

Let me always see the world You created through a lens of gratefulness.

I'm so thankful for all the people you've brought into my life. Help me show them just how much they mean to me.

AMEN.

What is any easy thing to be grateful for? What is a more difficult thing to be grateful for?

_____

_____

_____

_____

How do you incorporate gratefulness into your life? Are there times this is easier to do?

_____

_____

_____

_____

Who is someone you are grateful for? Do they know how much they mean to you?

_____

_____

_____

_____

Maybe it's the mom that welcomed you on the playground with your young kids....

The compliment from the stranger when life was moving too fast....

The timing of a friend when your grief couldn't get you out of the car....

So many moments and people touch our lives everyday expressing gratitude is easy in words, but what about action?

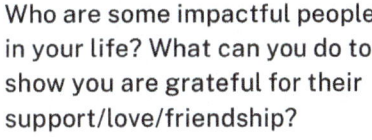

Who are some impactful people in your life? What can you do to show you are grateful for their support/love/friendship?

keychains inspired by @colormadehappy mailed with handwritten cards

you are
WORTHY

Chapter Seven

I Am Worthy

I used to think that a mid-life crisis – even a quarter-life crisis – was cliché. A drastic change, a new focus, it all seemed unnecessary. Those people lacked discipline, drive. How truly naive looking back now.

Sometimes the "crisis" doesn't come in the form of a new car or career, but a slow progressive shift in a new stage of life (and this part may be cliché). But as a flower slowly opens its petals to reveal a bloom, so do we to the new layers of ourselves we discover. We realize as we grow into adulthood that we don't depart from our old self but gain wisdom to take along for the years to come.

From early in my life, worth – and especially self-worth – was tied to accomplishment. Producing, achieving, ranking and gaining were what garnered the word "love." On my wedding night, my dad said during our father-daughter dance, "I'm so proud of you." Of course, the meaning was "I love you," but the words said *I'm proud you took this step*, *I'm proud of your choice*. The result, the action was the source of pride – not the qualities that led me to that decision, that night, my future.

Pride, when tied to external and worldly deeds, leaves one feeling empty. You can't ever "be enough." There would be no amount of accolades or promotions you could receive to ever feel worthy.

It's almost as if the path is set out so clearly that you don't have a chance to veer – graduate with honors, attend college, respectable career, marriage, kids...

With such a firm course, there's no room to ask, *Who am I as a person? What do I like to do? What's next after the prescribed steps? Where does my worth come from?*

Our worth is in the Lord.

> "Do not fear, for I have redeemed you; I have summoned
> you by name; you are Mine." (Isaiah 43:1)

It really is that simple. Seeing that I am His, made in His image, I am worthy of the kingdom. Jesus died for me (whether I did all the prescribed steps, did them in order, or charted my own course).

A change, an alignment of priorities, a new way of living takes courage, passion, and motivation. It takes knowing that what you're used to isn't what you want. They were the ones making their path.

Questioning, sitting with uncomfortable feelings, and wrestling with your worth can all feel wrong – but realizing that you are absolutely worthy in His eyes because you know where your worth comes from, that feels pretty right.

God, **You are where my worth lies**. Not in worldly goods or deeds.

Help me to always remember this especially when going after "the next big thing." Lead my heart back to You.

Let me be a proud model of charting a course because of You so that others may see, question, and follow You also.

AMEN.

What does self-worth mean to you? How have you felt it or demonstrated it in your life?

_____

_____

_____

When we feel ourselves going after "the next thing," what can we use to call ourselves back and focus our attention?

_____

_____

_____

What examples of trailblazers of faith do you know? What makes them unique?

_____

_____

_____

When's the last time you wore something so totally you?

A rainbow bedazzled hat (made 10 min before an event!)

A rainbow sequin jacket that just shines!

A pair of glitter sneakers for any travel adventure

Sometimes it's the quiet voice that speaks your true desires - they may go against the grain.

Remember we're done with prescribed steps - we know where our worth lies.

What would be your signature piece?
Think even outside of clothes - jewelry, shoes, a specific color, makeup style, hair color or style.

Choose one thing to fulfill a secret wish or desire you thought was too "wild."

you are
STRONG

Chapter Eight

I am Strong

Strong definitely doesn't seem like a word to describe me in any of its definitions. It seems reserved for someone with big muscles exuding leadership with a commanding personality and maybe a voice to match. Strong isn't even synonymous with most of the women I consider role models.

It's almost as if I'd be afraid to be called strong. There's a pressure that comes with being "strong," a standard to live up to and a weight of being unbreakable.

Here's what I've learned about strength. Strength isn't an "all the time" quality. **It is in the little decisions**.

...standing by a friend when they have an impossible decision to make.

...holding it together and still showing vulnerability when grief is drowning you.

...finally accepting help after struggling. Realizing that falling into the arms of those who love you can carry you through a tough time.

Not long ago, I struggled with my job. I would cry, not knowing why, for weeks, feeling lost and stressed. I tried to "happy my way through it." I did things to uplift others in the office – dressing up in inflatable costumes, candy with positive notes, unexpected surprises awaiting coworkers. It almost felt like the more I did for others, the less happy I was. It was a weird way of coping that didn't fix any underlying issues.

I made an appointment with a counselor to get help. I wanted to be "the old me" who I knew didn't used to live this way or was better able to cope. I got tools to improve my thinking, to proactively work to keep myself in a better place and a safe place to grow.

Even admitting to seeing a counselor still feels triggering with so much stigma on mental health. I was scared to tell people I went, that I still go, that I hold space for this important part of my health and well-being. Some of my close circle knew, and eventually because I felt more comfortable sharing, others around me sought out help as well. It sure didn't feel strong in that moment. It felt weak. I felt broken and lost with very few options.

But I was strong to reach out and accept help. I was strong to share and advocate for others who could benefit. In Psalm 28:7 we hear,

> "The Lord is my strength and my shield; my heart trusts in Him, and He helps me."

We all fight battles in different ways, whether it be with pure strength, mighty prayer, or tiny decisions. We can know where our strength lies and who to call on in times of distress. At first I thought strong looked like going it alone. Now I know strong looks like accepting help from others, advocating for yourself, perseverance, and the quiet unending prayer for God to keep us on our path.

God, You are my strength!

When I feel weak, broken or lost - keep me in the path You have laid out for me.

Keep my heart in prayer and my eyes open to all resources and people You have placed in my life.

Help me feel strong in what is important - Your word and leading others to it.

AMEN.

What is a moment in your life you felt strong? What would be your definition of strength?

_____

_____

_____

Has your definition of strong role models changed over your life?

_____

_____

_____

Where are examples of strength you remember from the Bible?

_____

_____

_____

These two quotes hang right next to religious artwork in our dining room. Reminding me of other strong individuals in our lives.

I actually right names on the picture to the left of people who left a huge impression on my life and invite my family to do the same.

This song keeps my focus on my family who I hold so close

Copies of these are in the Templates section.!

God is our refuge
and strength, an
ever-present help
in distress

PSALM 46:1

you are
CALM

Chapter Nine

I Am Calm

Sometimes we have to work backwards. I almost titled this chapter "I am 'the opposite of anxious/worried.'" At least that's the goal.

This is one I'm constantly working on. I am a most anxious person. I live in the 50 worst scenarios around every single situation. I drown myself in thoughts about safety and rely on others' moods to gauge how I, myself, am feeling. I really struggle with embracing the present and looking forward to the future with hopeful eyes instead of controlling fear.

Right after we were married, my husband and I moved to a small Minnesota town for him to finish his degree. I found a job teaching kindergarten, but nothing really prepares you for the first Minnesota winter. The snow drifts up to and almost covering our first floor apartment windows. The negative double-digit wind chills for weeks and learning the saying "too cold to snow." The white-out conditions when snow doesn't melt but blows viciously over the flat land.....so homey, right?

While it wasn't something I was used to, everyone else was. I learned of new sports and winter activities that many people loved.

My parents, godmother, and cousin came to visit in the middle of that first brutal winter and my husband, being the great host he is, thought we should see the frozen lake. After all, ice fishing is a sport. People put up houses (and even get pizza delivered to them!). So we were driving along and I said, "Up ahead is where it's normally water." My husband noted, "Nope, we're on the lake."

Alarm bells! *We're already on the lake? Like driving on the water? The one we walked around a few months ago?* My apparently much more south Midwestern brain couldn't quite comprehend it; all winter up until that point, I'd been saying it wasn't safe to go out on the frozen lake. And here we were driving on it, not sinking, exploring the ice houses as they were lined up to form a mini town with streets. We even stopped and got a tour of one.

The chance to let go and be brave offered a new perspective. A lesson that otherwise would have kept me in my safe shell for eternity. Sometimes we get a push; sometimes we are the push.

I won't make the walking on water reference, although it would be easy, but I do fondly remember that time crossing what I thought to be a treacherous path only to be pretty excited and calm after the initial shock. Just taking a step back, getting that perspective can make all the difference.

Just like we read in Luke 12:25:

"Who of you by worrying can add a single hour to your life?"

We sure won't be able to _add_ any time to our lives worrying but we could _lose_ a lot of time. My grandma passed along this wisdom my cousin shared with me: "Give it to God." When it's all in His hands, all our fears, worries, concerns—we are calm.

Help me feel the quiet calm only found in You. Keep my eyes focused on the present and let my heart rest in knowing You have it covered.

When I feel the familiar pull of tomorrow - ground me in today.

Show me the way to model taking things pieces at a time since You are all I need.

AMEN.

What is a time in your life that you felt calm/peace? Are there specific conditions that you could replicate

_____
_____
_____
_____

In what situations are we called to be calm? How can you model this for others?

_____
_____
_____
_____

Does calm mean you are in control of your emotions? why or why not?

_____
_____
_____
_____

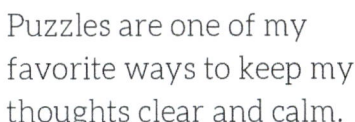

Puzzles are one of my favorite ways to keep my thoughts clear and calm.

I am obsessed with Disney Thomas Kinkaid puzzles. (specifically 500 piece that fit on our dining room table and take minimal time to complete)

Another great gift or idea is capturing family memories as puzzles.

They are relatively inexpensive and puzzles are the best parallel play. Great to do together to talk, mingle, and enjoy company at the same time.

What's a memory that you would love to piece together?

Who would you love to spend time with calmly crafting?

you are
HELPFUL

Chapter Ten

I am Helpful

Most often help is not thought about and is just immediate. A close coworker of mine passed away, and I worked in the same building as my sister-in-law at the time. It was in no way a coincidence that on the very morning I was to come back to work we arrived and parked close to each other in the parking garage. I was in my car thinking, *I'm not sure how to get there. How do I walk past that desk? This path isn't the same anymore*. My sister-in-law walked me in and kept my spirits up; without her, I'd have no doubt just called in sick from the parking garage.

Sometimes help looks different. I like to think of myself as a helpful person—available, supportive, generous, kind—but when I look deep inside, sometimes I mistake help for control.

I want to help so I can control the outcome or the perception of me, which discredits my intentions. True help if I'm able to give it, should be flexible and centered on what the recipient expressly needs or has asked for – not what I deem helpful.

When hearing about a family tragedy, a friend's loss, or a pandemic in the world, my mind jumps to help. If my hands can make food or heal with words, I want to go and do and fix. Sometimes it just helps me heal, though – maybe the recipient didn't need another casserole or freezer meal. They needed space and time to speak about their loss. They didn't need a "things you may not have thought of" list for their big event – they just needed a safe space to speak about the upcoming nuptials.

I jump quickly and solidly to fixing mode rather than sitting alone with how I feel. My intentions are good and honest but might not truly be helpful.

Do I want to be seen as helpful or felt as helpful? Am I doing this because it's "proper" or expected, or because I think it will lessen a burden, OR has the recipient specifically asked for help in this way.

Giving the recipient options of what you could do is a great way to leave the decision to them. And I have to remember to not offer advice unless I'm asked to—it blows my mind, because I really feel like I'm helping, but it might not be a focus and it would only serve to control the outcome.

Proverbs 3:27 says,

> "Do not withhold good from those to whom it is due, when it is in your power to act."

Help, while seemingly smooth and easy, is one I often find myself questioning. This prayer keeps God's will as a focus for my intentions.

God, show me how to help and love others just as You do.

Keep my intentions pure and focused on how best I can serve, especially when my mind jumps to solving mode. Help me learn to accept help from those special people You put in my life.

Lead me to show up for others as an example of Your love and point them to You.

AMEN.

Think back to a time someone meaningfully helped you - what made that moment stick out? Why were you touched?

What does that tell you about yourself?

What are some ideas of help (not control!) you have for more routine situations (death in family, new parent, event, moving)

What does help look like for you? Do you accept help easily or are you able to ask?

Any true help I feel I've offered and that is best accepted is not tangible, but there is a way to "craft" our help if you will to best meet the needs of others.

Here are some real scripts and tricks to use when you are in a position to help another.

The most important part is leaning in with their feelings not fixing or adding to their burden.

For grief, tough times, not sure what to say:

- "I'm hear to listen"
- "No reply needed, I'm thinking of you as ...."
- "Remember when...(share a memory you want them to know you treasure)"
- "I don't have words, but I do love you."
- "I'm here for you however you need me"
- "How are things this morning/holiday?" (Remembering this can be a long term)
- Accept silence - don't burden with continued offers of help

For times you really want to offer help, choose some suggestions and let the recipient decide:

- "I'd love to send you dinner from your fave restaurant or bring over something homemade, what date works best?"
- "I can watch your children from ___ and get them fed and bring them back at _____."
- "I can send prayers your way <3"
- "I can grab your grocery order and leave it on your porch - no talking required."
- "I can sit and listen."
- "I can clean while you are out of your house."
- "I can run errands for or with you."

Tailor the offer to your gifts! It takes the thinking out of it on their part and provides tangible choice in what help or support best looks like!

- Do you love to cook? Have a favorite recipe?
- Organization your thing? - offer to help with moving, new baby clothes, kitchen remodels,
- personal experience with the same type of issue? listen and empathizing from a similar perspective
- Entertaining your forte? Offer to babysit, throw a get out of the house party, or help with party prep for someone's event

you are
MERRY

Chapter Eleven

I Am Merry

You can't think of the word *merry* without that slight smile that lifts up just half your mouth, the one that if anyone else saw they would think you have a secret.

Merry is filled to the brim with bubbles and joining with others in overflowing happiness. Sharing laughter, enjoying company, and gathering for a meal (not even just holidays) all come to mind when you think of merry times.

I loved jokes as a kid (still do!) and had a binder where I would cut my favorites out of books and share them with family around our summer campfires. I love making people laugh. Even though comedian wasn't in the life plan as a career, I still love appreciating and capturing those merry moments as they happen.

This moment still has me smiling and laughing as I think about it. Our house only has one bathroom. The bathroom is located next to our "master" bedroom. Our four-year-old son has always, always woken up early. He's an early riser, and this morning was no exception. His routine is to immediately run to the bathroom, then he goes to play quietly in our family room after letting us know he's up.

At 5:30 a.m. on this glorious morning, we wake up to "...and he will RAISE YOU UP on the LAST DAY," being belted from the bathroom. This might be a familiar hymn titled, "On Eagle's Wings," except at this decibel level and with more of a rock tempo it would not be something that would be coming up in church anytime soon. I turn to my husband and ask, "Is he singing what I think he's singing? Is it the rock version?" We dissolved into laughter while also shaking our heads, not quite believing this was the *alarm* for our day.

The pure unexpected shock and the laughter brought connection and merriment to the day.

Laughter might not traditionally be thought of as a gift, but I think differently. **Laughter brings people together.** Not just families either—coworkers, friends, distant relatives, concertgoers and so many more. It brings light to situations and gives common ground when you find the same things funny as another person.

In chapters 17-18 of Genesis, laughter is mentioned five times when Abraham and Sarah learn they're pregnant – more than in any other story in the Bible. To me this correlates well with the expression, "If you want to hear God laugh, tell him your plans." In Genesis 21:6 we read,

> "Sarah said, 'God has brought me laughter, and everyone who hears about this will laugh with me.'"

If the sound and feeling of laughter is something I can bring the world, don't let me hold back.

God, help me see You in those merry moments.

Keep my heart light as I navigate through a world full of darkness and despair.

Show me places to bring joy and laughter to those around me. With unexpected smiles, shared laughs, and common joys bring people to my life that keep merriment at the forefront.

AMEN.

Who do you know that makes you laugh? What characteristics or situations do you think contribute to this?

_____

_____

_____

What are some ways to inspire or create positive laughter?

_____

_____

_____

Does laughter bring us closer to God? If so, how? Share examples from your own life.

_____

_____

_____

Sometimes merry is showing up at work in inflatable costumes -
perusing around, passing out candy like a parade. Surprised but
smiling coworkers welcomed our crazy endeavor.

The unexpected joy just shows up in crazy places sometimes.....

Have you witnessed merriment in an unexpected place??

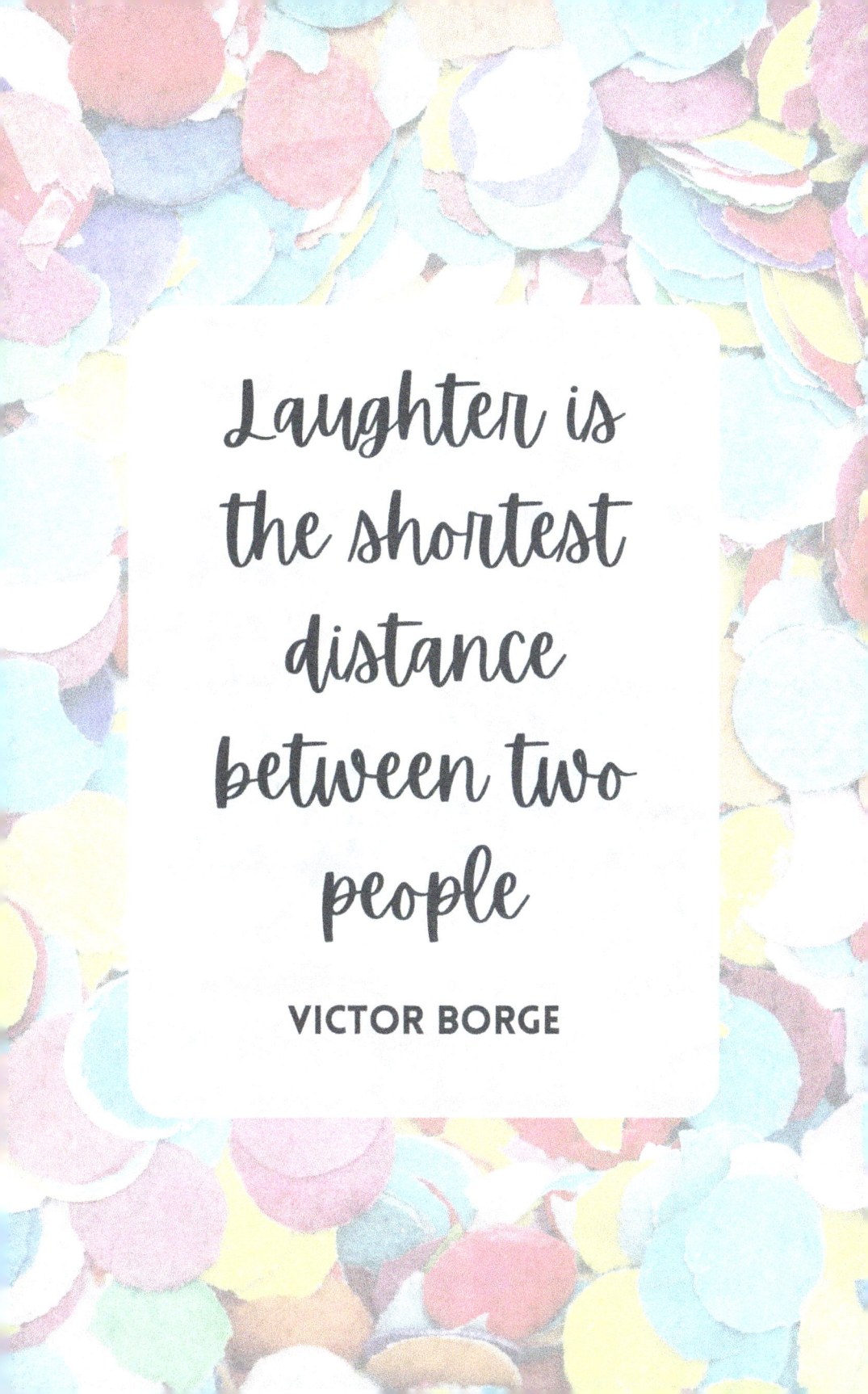

Laughter is
the shortest
distance
between two
people

VICTOR BORGE

you are
KIND

Chapter Twelve

I Am Kind

Two powerful women in my life are models of kindness—my mother and my mother-in-law.

After the birth of our first son, I was more than a little lost. Pushing myself to be strong and feeling like I should know how to do handle a baby 24/7 while recovering from birth and multiple infections was too much. In the midst of caring for the baby, I didn't know how to be a mom, and the learning curve was steep! The joy of new life was marred with moments of struggle, indecision, questioning, and loneliness.

I would think, *This happens all the time, every mother goes through these feelings,* and it would still all shake out to, *Why do I feel this way? Is something wrong with me?*

My mom came over nearly every day of my maternity leave—to keep me company, to help me figure out this new mom routine, to give me guilt-free time to bathe, and to keep us all fed. For so long, I thought about how weak I was, how much I struggled, how things seemed so different than I thought they would be. I look back now with a *drastically* different view. My mom knew, even when I didn't ask for help, how she could be there. She knew from her own experience how to support me. She was kind when I wasn't kind to myself, when I wasn't giving myself near enough grace.

There are no words to describe the selflessness, compassion, and generous spirit my mother-in-law has.

After COVID hit and our world turned upside down with two little boys, she was a light in the darkness. With few places of safety or anywhere to really get outside the house with energetic youngsters, her house became one of reprieve.

As a parent of young kids, it's always a treasure to have a place that's child-proofed—the house, the yard, all of it. Exploration abounds, and we can get our wiggles out at grandmas. With a listening ear, an offer to watch the kids so I could get a treasured walk alone, we had a safe space that all of us could be in. Like a final sigh of relief at the end of a long day, grandma's house was our escape where the sun shone just a little brighter, you could let your hair down, and the expectations of the world just didn't seem as heavy.

We **recognize kindness everyday** in little moments of door holding, smiles of encouragement, or thank-you notes. Sometimes we overlook the sustained intentional efforts of those close to us and the beautiful kind role models they provide for us. In Ephesians 4:32 we hear directly,

"Be kind to one another."

No matter how it shows up in our lives—small pure moments, treasured relationships, or even tough conversations—kindness files at the hard edges in our life and smooths our course.

God, let me see Your kindness everyday.

I want to **show kindness in my thoughts, words, and actions**. Whether little or big, let my actions point to You.

Teach me how to recognize all the kind hearts You put in my life.

AMEN.

What is a time in your life that someone's kindness touched you?

_____

_____

_____

_____

What are some ideas you have for working with those who feel the most difficult to be kind towards?

_____

_____

_____

_____

What examples of kindness have you read about in the Bible? What are ones that stick out or you remember?

_____

_____

_____

_____

I think kindness is intentional in some ways. The act of thinking and choosing versus spur of the moment.

Since COVID, our family hosts an Act of Kindness week. We pick a traditionally slower time (end of winter almost spring) and research, discuss and brainstorm all the people we can show kindness to in that week.

The picture above was when our family baked truffles and packaged them. Each truffle had acts of kindness that person or family could do to pay it forward as well.

Here's a few ideas we've done in past:

- delivering flowers
- fresh donuts to grandparents
- wrote letters and mailed pictures or lottery tickets
- online shopped for new parents
- teacher favorites delivered during the week
- frozen meals or Door Dash for close friends

Oatmeal Butterscotch Truffles

1/2 cup butter, softened
1/2 cup brown sugar
1/4 cup granulated sugar
3-4 Tbsp. milk
1/2 tsp vanilla
3/4 cup flour
1/2 tsp. cinnamon
1/4 tsp. salt
1 1/2 cup oats
1 cup butterscotch chips
1 package white almond bark

Cream together butter and sugars. Add milk, and vanilla. Add flour, cinnamon, and salt. Mix in oats. Finely chop butterscotch chips and add in.

Roll into balls and put onto wax lined sheet. Refrigerate 30 min. Melt half of the almond bark in 30 second increments until melted. Dip each ball and place on sheet. Chill until hardened.

My granmda's trademark cookie is an "Oatmeal Scotchie" and these were just perfect. You could probably add butterscotch pudding mix too (....shhh that was the secret for the moist cookies)

If you had a Kindness Week - list some people you'd love to bless, things you'd love to do (your talents)

you are
FORGIVEN

Chapter Thirteen

I Am Forgiven

Forgiveness is sometimes hard to speak, but profoundly important. I grew up in a family where forgiveness was more or less implied and guilt was the traditional motivator of faith. There might have been "I'm sorry," but nothing much after that.

I learned more about forgiveness through one short event than I had in my entire life.

When I was a new mom of two young boys, church was an event – dressing up in "church clothes," getting out the door on time, filing in and keeping quiet for an extended amount of time. It was crushing on my anxiety and I felt lost, not hearing most of the service or the sermon because I was attending to my children's needs.

One friend I remember texting during that time noted, "This is where God wants you. This stage is just about coming and not listening. Just absorb the community and togetherness as you show examples to your children." That did provide comfort for a while, but it was still hard.

After one service concluded, our pastor mentioned the kids and the noise level. (It's important to note here that the pastor is my father-in-law.) I was crushed. I tried so hard to be there, to survive, really, during the service, giving it all I had. I just knew he had to be speaking to me. I took it as an attack on my parenting skills and our disruption to the congregation.

I left defeated. My husband brought it up to his dad just explaining how I felt. A few days later I was chatting in a coworkers office and I heard the pastor's voice. This was definitely odd, as he had never visited before and it was a large office. You'd have to ask someone to find my cubicle, so the chances of him just stopping by were slim. What was he doing there?

He opened his palm and offered me a decorative porcupine with **"I'm so sorry. Please forgive me"** written on the bottom. He explained his reasoning—that kids are the lifeblood of churches and their excitement and noise is not viewed as negative. We hugged. There may have been tears. Of course, I forgave him.

Two things stick out to me.

1. Rarely do we follow "I'm sorry" with forgiveness. But it's so important to feel it in our hearts and model it for others. When we're already admitting something or acknowledging and having to follow it up with an ask seems very vulnerable.

2. He went out of his way to make sure I knew in person that this meant a great deal to him.

Our human condition lends itself naturally to misunderstandings and miscommunication. We're flawed. We read in 1 Corinthians 15:3:

"Christ died for our sins according to the Scriptures."

When I reflect on our salvation with all our sins forgiven—I see those exact two things. First it's not only that we're sorry but we're forgiven. The weight of our sins wiped out completely. Second, Jesus models for us in the Bible that he would do this for us. It means a great deal to him.

Maybe you see these little examples. We all sin, so this comes up frequently. Reflecting on our biblical model of forgiveness points us in the right direction.

God, open my heart to forgive others. Let me
 embrace vulnerability admitting when I've
been wrong.

Open my eyes to examples of forgiveness I see
- just like the model You are for us.

When forgiveness feels hard, help me to **be
brave**.

AMEN.

What does forgiving someone feel like in your heart?
What does being forgiven feel like?

_____

_____

_____

_____

What do you think the term "the **power** of forgiveness" means?

_____

_____

_____

_____

Have you witnessed or had experience with the power of forgiveness?

_____

_____

_____

_____

The porcupine sits at every work desk as a reminder. Forgiveness can be hard, a craft or food or note can be a great way to deliver when communication is tough.

Think about what means most to the person and what your small gift could convey.

If you love baking......a sweet they rarely get to indulge in
If you love crafts.....a painting or key chain with their favorite colors
If you're sentimental.....a favorite picture of you together or a special note
If you have time......a snack, coffee, or flowers delivered to them

you are
UNIFYING

Chapter Fourteen

I Am Unifying

Bringing people together, crafting experiences that are seared into memory is one of my absolute favorite things to do.

From an early age, I was able to see this model as families gathered for special events and holidays. More than just watching and learning how to be a good host, I observed the development and planning that goes into events. Knowing the ages of everyone coming and providing space and places for gathering, while having open-ended activities, made the event successful.

On the flip side, carving out time to attend events shows the message of importance and that we care. We had time to build relationships and grow closer to those we saw most often.

In my family, both of my grandmothers can be viewed as matriarchs, the axis that our family spun around. They were the gathering place, the organizers, the food providers. If our family was a garden, they were the ones watering, nourishing and giving space so we all could grow.

Maybe not all my memories over the years directly involved them, but they were behind the scenes. They made sure everything was in place for the memories to be made—people were together, often sharing food, playing (outside or inside). Their houses almost physically feel like a hug – just from the sheer amount of time spent and special moments that happened there.

The time spent leads to memories made and ultimately to tradition that my family cherishes.

We do an annual cookie bake, with some years exceeding 1,000 cookies. With our large extended family, this has always been a truly special time of togetherness, fun and enjoyment. The tradition continues to buoy and sustain connections, even as we lost our matriarch in 2020.

Even small traditions in our own household like putting up the Christmas tree (after Halloween), or all of us wearing onesies during December for a fun movie/snack party, build our family bonds.

In Hebrews 10:25 we read,

> "...not giving up meeting together, as some are in the habit of doing, but encouraging one another—and all the more as you see the Day approaching."

While we gather together in church and encourage one another weekly, this can also mean reaching out to others and bringing them together. Bringing people closer leads to relationship and modeling life as a Christian.

I think back to the the women who did that for our family, unifying us and helping us grow so we in turn could do the same for others—bring them into the fold by spending time together and forging bonds.

God, help me bring people together and encourage them.

Use me as model and a unifier to help others build, create, and strengthen their relationships as Christians.

Keep the focus on You and Your Word.

AMEN.

In what ways has being with a group (in any capacity) strengthened your faith?

_____

_____

_____

_____

What traditions or memories do you hold dear (doesn't have to be family!)?

What are ones you hope to create or pass on?

_____

_____

_____

_____

Where do we see examples of unifying in the Bible? What do you take away from them?

_____

_____

_____

_____

Combine what you like to do with available space and invite people who share or want to learn more

Think of things you love to do:

- try new foods/restaurants
- book club
- crafting
- games
- entertaining
-
-

What space do you have available?

- your house
- park
- community center
- local community events (check social media for events in your area)
-
-

Here are some ideas we've done in the past:

- Sushi night
- eating spaghetti off the table
- Olympic themed games with friends
- card and crafting making with family
- campouts
- Marriage Nights at church
- Disney karaoke
- game nights

For where two or three gather in My name, I am there with them

you are
OBSERVANT

Chapter Fifteen

I Am Observant

Once I was attending a lunch with two former coworkers. They filled up my heart, and I left feeling so light. I walked right out of the restaurant and marched over to my red van.

I hopped in the driver's seat and noticed my laptop bag was missing! A new job with a missing laptop...and it was only a few months before that my purse was stolen. My heart dropped into my stomach. The dread was palpable. After hanging my head, I looked up to see another red van directly in front of me. I quickly turned around and saw that the back of the van I was in *definitely* did not look like kids had invaded. I was in the wrong vehicle.

I quickly jumped out and back into my own before the owner came. Relief washed over me, but the adrenaline was pumping.

While this incident does not show me to be an observant person, **observant to me means more than just with the eyes.** You need your ears to listen, your heart to understand and your hands to do. Being observant means noticing the details, cataloging the words and ideas that help build relationships.

It can mean jotting down gift ideas for for a relative or friend.

It can be noticing a change in text or voice when a close companion may be struggling.

It can be seeing a shift in behavior of a coworker who may need help.

When you're observant it comes out in the way you treat and interact with other people. You notice more. You build trust over shared details and remembered stories. Being observant means slowing down and processing information after you take it in. Thinking back to how the conversation played out, words that were said, what body language was used.

It's usually easiest to be observant of those we see daily. The moods of our partner, kids and coworkers can be seen and "read" quickly, as we know them. When we spend time with family, friends, or acquaintances listening and observing are crucial. I like asking deeper questions such as:

- What are you looking forward to coming up?

- How did your last _____ (craft...sporting event....hobby....family gathering) go?

- Have you done anymore with _____ (shared interest)?

- You've always been _____ (a trait you admire), and I admire that about you. What's your secret?

These get you away from the weather and other surface-level topics and allow you to establish or build on common interests.

We hear about being observant in the Bible as "keeping alert" or,

"Be on your guard; stand firm in the faith; be courageous; be strong." (1 Corinthians 16:13)

We can use this gift to stand ready, not only for Judgement Day but to build up others around us. Notice how we can help. See where we can bring others' up. Observe where our other gifts can be put to use.

God, help me to be observant.

Use my eyes, my ears, my heart and my hands to do Your will.

I want to notice where I can do more. I want to be an example for others of jumping in even when it feels hard.

Show me the way to see and serve like You.

AMEN.

Eyes, hands, heart, ears, where do you see the biggest opportunity to improve being observant?

_____

_____

_____

What examples can you recall of someone noticing or being noticed in the Bible? What can those examples tell us about observation?

_____

_____

_____

Recall a time someone noticed you in a positive way (anything except for your physical appearance) - how did it make you feel? How can we use this to model for others in our life?

_____

_____

_____

Being observant really lends itself to gift giving.

A custom eyeshadow palette for their eye color while naming the shadows based on places they love.

I love paint by number pictures of a treasured photo - such a great gift!

When you know someone's likes, interests and traits - you can anticipate how to brighten their day, put a smile on their face, and a feeling in their heart that you care.

Take time to notice ....even if your notes in end up in the app on your phone or a folded list in your purse - it's worth it!!

you are
TRADITIONAL

Chapter Sixteen

I Am Traditional

Did you inwardly cringe seeing this word? Did it make you feel outdated? Did it conjure up an old relative's house with decorations of yesteryear?

Tradition is multi-faceted. I think about tradition as everyone having a string that will end but gets tied to others all along the way...stories, activities, items are all passed down. The strings all continue intertwining into the fabric of our culture laced with history.

The beauty is in the choice. What will I keep? What traditions does my family value from our past? What do we want to make or pass down to others? Instead of seeing "what we always do," what values can this tradition bring that I want to continue?

Santa, Elf on the Shelf, the Tooth Fairy, the Easter Bunny...none of these exist in our home as part of our holiday traditions. This was a decision my husband and I made early in our marriage. I was brought up with these holiday figures, and he wasn't. We discussed all the benefits (no mad rush to put gifts out Christmas Eve!) and pitfalls (explaining to other family members). We made the choice that fit our family, and we haven't looked back.

We open up gifts all throughout December and take time to relish in each one with lots of focus on new books, games and family memories. We savor Christmas day in church and celebrate our Savior's birth.

Some traditions we keep and look forward to. They serve our family well.

We vacation every Memorial Day to the same "retreat" on Bull Shoals Lake. Cabins lining a gravel drive with a gorgeous lake view. Space for us all to spread out and yet simultaneously be all together. An abundance of activities for every age level. The memories of this nearly 25+ year pilgrimage are so cherished. The fact that I'm able to bring my kids to the same place I would go each year is hard to comprehend. Each year when we leave, I cry because we won't return for another year, and I know just how special the bonds and the place truly are. I have yet to find another location that comes close to the peace and serenity of this place that allows me to truly "let go."

Those traditions, the ones that you hold close and easily plan around – those are the ones worth keeping. They add to your life. They give you something to look forward to. Little bright spots or stars in a long calendar year.

Traditions have to start somewhere. You may already have some with your family or friends, or you may have some you could start. Some old, some new—all carefully chosen woven into the tapestry of our culture. Even Jesus' disciples were questioned on tradition, as the Pharisees noted that they did not wash their hands before they ate. Jesus replied by asking them,

> "And why do you break the command of God for the sake of your tradition?" (Matthew 15:3)

In faith, we can explore and pursue traditions that reflect God's commandments.

God, I see all the beautiful traditions set before me - in church, in our families, in our cultures. **Help me to discern what is best.**

Show me what to keep and what can help turn more people to You.

Lead me as a voice of change if it is Your will. Keep my heart set on serving You.

AMEN.

What is an example of a tradition you keep?
What is an example of a tradition you decided against?

_____

_____

_____

_____

Have you felt pressure to keep doing things they way
they have been done? How do you embrace change or
suggest for others?

_____

_____

_____

_____

In what ways could you incorporate others into your
traditions to strengthen relationships?

_____

_____

_____

_____

Baking is a traditional activity for our family. My grandma started the tradition of baking cookies for our huge extended family to decorate and take home.

This apron was made with fabric leftover from wedding projects and custom fabric (ordered through Spoonflower) with a collage of recipes from my favorite family cooks. The recipes in each person's own writing are close to me when I use it.

Traditions can be creative and bring in fun elements! **What can you create to elevate your traditions?**

you are
RESTFUL

Chapter Seventeen

I am Restful

The goal is not to go at 100% capacity 100% of the time. Machines break down. Bodies and minds crumble under pressure. I don't know about you, but for me, rest sure feels guilty. I feel more restless than restful.

Take a break?! Not with one million things coming up. Not when everyone else is working. Not when my body tells me to.

Part of functioning, thinking, and being our best is resting. It has to be in there—and not just the sleeping part, but space to let your mind wander, dream, think, plan and just BE. How minimal is that time in a crazy, hectic, "always going" world?

I like to remind myself of times I did value rest and the great outcomes. Once when we were visiting friends in Montana, my husband and I hiked up a trail to watch the sunrise. This is pretty out of character for us; we're early risers but there aren't many places to hike where we live.

There were many people on the trail so we felt confident heading up. Although we only made it part of the way, it was truly surreal to watch the sun inch over the horizon and cascade down into the valley. It felt like slow motion, but pretty quickly the world was light. The city in the valley awakening for the new day. **The peace, the calm, the rest in just being in that moment** has really stayed with me. Upon subsequent travels like in the Smoky Mountains we did the same thing, watching the magnificent colors as the sky transformed from purple to blue lighter and lighter until it was as if darkness never existed.

Time stands still in those moments.

Sometimes rest is forced. After a surgery or during an illness, it's necessary to heal and recover.

Sometimes rest is needed. A break in a heated argument, when you can come back level headed.

Resting is naturally a great time for prayer. We see many Biblical references to rest—an entire day in the Creation story, which led to the custom of resting on the Sabbath. In Matthew 11:28 we hear,

> "Come to me, all you who are weary and burdened, and
> I will give you rest."

How often does our day-to-day feel burdened by the endless "to-do"s and needs of others? Just like *Mercy Me* sings, "The fight's already been won. That's the best news ever."

I find comfort in my forever home, knowing that during this weary, burdensome, restless life, I can find rest in our Savior.

God, when I feel restless, help me to seek You.

Keep me from the endless running of keeping up with the ideal of success.

Keep my heart at rest with You as my focus. Show me to live as an example for others that they might come to You.

Help me to remember how crucial rest is and to make time to rest with You in prayer.

AMEN.

Where do you find rest physically? emotionally? spiritually?

In what ways can you be a positive example to show rest is important?

What does true rest feel like in your body? Do you have any "markers" to help determine you are rested or that you need rest?

Little things for people that make them proud of what they have done

Embroidery has to be one of the most restful crafts! Easy to take along, so fun to personalize!

The middle picture is a quote from my in laws wedding song they wrote, a replica bouquet , and the flowers above are the birthstones of all their children.

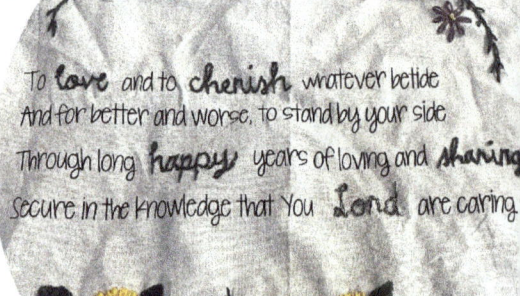

To love and to cherish whatever betide
And for better and worse, to stand by your side
Through long happy years of loving and sharing
Secure in the knowledge that You Lord are caring

The needle pushing through the fabric, the pulling of the thread, all keep your hands focused but your mind calm and present.

You can add color, texture, pictures and more.

It's a quiet craft that keeps your mind quiet too.

What could you add to your home or make for someone?

Drop your shoulders

Unclench your jaw

Remove your tongue
from the roof your
mouth

Deep Breath

Permission to rest

you are
LIGHTHEARTED

Chapter Eighteen

I Am Lighthearted

Even the word *lighthearted* makes me smile—cheerful, carefree, amusing, entertaining. I may not live up to this all the time but I sure feel it most of the time.

There are just times life can't be taken too seriously. You just have to smile, nod and make the best of it. I'm sure we all have a story that comes to mind—that you can maybe laugh and smile about now.

After the birth of our first child, going anywhere was like pushing a boulder uphill. You could pack a diaper bag, remember the car seat, get yourself ready and still forget extra clothes or formula. Our first doctor's appointment at two days old, we forgot the diaper bag altogether and my mom ran back to the house to grab it while we were inside. I remember feeling like such a failure as I tried to hold everything in my mind and things kept slipping out.

Getting our son ready for an outing a month or two later, he had a blowout as we were heading out the door. I always prided myself on being on time or early, but throwing children in the mix really took a toll. I looked him over and assessed my limited options. I could unsnap the onesie and pull it over him, but that could lead to spreading things everywhere. There might have to be a bath involved leading to extra time. My brilliant in-the-moment mind reached for scissors. I cut the bottom of the onesie off without so much as thinking. It cleaned up much easier and quicker. We had plenty of other outfits, but most of my family was horrified when I told them that story.

I also didn't realize that the shoulders of onesies "with the flap" you can roll down their bodies anyway. That sure would have been nice to know!

We made it work. I felt ok solving my parent crisis quickly and in a way that felt satisfactory. Looking back, it might have been a little unconventional, but I also didn't let the moment ruin my mood.

Coincidentally, another moment with scissors also lives in fame in our family.

My husband was braiding my hair. He grew up with sisters, so he has this talent. He told me to, "Hold on a sec," and I thought he was reaching for a bobby pin or hair tie. It was only when I heard the *snap* of the scissors that I realized he'd cut something. "Please tell me that was not my hair." It was only what didn't make it in the braid. His solution was to just trim it off.

Literally one ripple of shock went through my body, then laughter. It was amusing and solved the problem and didn't really affect the way I looked. Anytime that story is told, though, the raised eyebrows and the looks we get are beyond words.

Let the moment be the moment. No need to make it bigger than it is. Let it wash right over you (easier said than done, I know). In Proverbs 31:25 we read,

> "She is clothed with strength and dignity; she can laugh at the days to come."

We have God behind us, beside us and before us. We can laugh at the little moments that come our way and try to deter us. We can remain calm and keep our focus.

God, **keep my heart light**.

Keep my heart cheerful and mind easygoing
 toward all life throws my way.

Let me be a model to others that small
moments don't have to be big moments and we
might even laugh about them later.

Help me keep reactions in check and You as
my focus.

AMEN.

Was there a time you had a big reaction to a small moment? Do you look different now?

_____
_____
_____
_____

In which situations can being lighthearted be helpful or beneficial? In which situations can it be detrimental?

_____
_____
_____
_____

Think of someone who comes to mind that is lighthearted - what about them do you enjoy?

_____
_____
_____
_____

I usually don't have any serious decor and these Disney paintings are my favorite! They've hung up in our nursery and now my office for years. Can you spot the newest edition?!

They could be viewed as juvenile but I love the color and magic they represent - a carry over from childhood if you will. The lighthearted films packed with inspiring messages are still ones I love to share with our kids today.

Other ways to bring some lightheartedness to our lives:
- eat spaghetti off the table (no utensils!)
- play games together - board games, video games, it all counts
- have a gas station trip (grab a fun snack or drink) .... when you live in the smallest town this is a big deal
- Backwards dinner - eat dessert first

Write your lighthearted ideas for home, family, friends here:

you are
PERSEVERING

Chapter Nineteen

I Am Persevering

A wise woman once told me being a human is the toughest job (getting along with othe comes in second). We aren't born knowing how to engage with others. We make mistakes and learn our whole lives as we grow older. Emotions, situations, relationships—all shift, ebb, and flow every day of our life. Then we have life events that catapult us into states of being that are new to us or ones we never thought we'd experience – a new baby, grief over a loved one, impossible circumstances.

Every storm runs out of rain. We know that platitude should help us but it sure doesn't soothe in the moment.

Once our family set out for a family vacation that would last a few days. For our first night, we had a campsite reserved. We had packed food, our tent, games, and we were ready to explore. We ended up lost on our way to the campground; with both our boys asleep in the back, we traversed a gravel road that we should have realized wasn't going to magically unfold into a glorious camping spot seven miles later.

When we got to our destination it was POURING rain. I mean wipers on blast, sheets of rain cascading and radar indication of it not stopping any time soon. We waited and waited for a time to pitch the tent that just never came. My husband got it up in the rain, but everything was wet inside. A warm fire to dry things out was out of the question. We used all the towels we had to make some dry space for us to be in the tent. We ended up going to get more towels and quarters so we could use the dryers to have dry clothing and blankets.

Especially when I'm driving in rain or storms, I try to remind myself, *You'll get out of this*. But that day it did not feel like we were catching a break. It was not a good start...BUT the next day it stopped. We were able to explore, find a playground, make smores and almost forget the entire "wet blanket" the previous day had been.

A first instinct is always to run or flee (a hotel room sounded pretty darn nice!) when faced with something large or uncomfortable, but I can do tough things. You can do tough things. We can stick it out. Some problems we can't run away from.

I don't want to make light of or minimize the struggles that each and every person encounters, but we need to keep our focus on His Word. These earthly problems won't last and we do have God with us to help us through. Reading the book of James, we see how trials can ultimately help us learn and grow:

> "Blessed is the one who perseveres under trial because, having stood the test, that person will receive the crown of life that the Lord has promised to those who love him." (James 1:12)

There are so many deeper, darker struggles that every person has—that most often they don't show. We can be tough AND tired, but we don't walk alone.

God, help me to persevere every day.

Through struggles and trials in my life, **show me I can get through with You** by my side.

Help me to show grace to others who are enduring hardships but to also lift them up. Guide me to show empathy as we all navigate through our sinful lives.

AMEN.

Is persevering a word you would use to describe yourself - why or why not.

Think of someone who might just be persevering, maybe in a "surviving not thriving" time - how can you be a light to them?

How does the word persevering change your frame of mind when experiencing a tough moment, situation, or time?

Persevering in crafts immediately made me think of quilting.

Huge projects in time, space, planning and bit by bit they come together.

The planning and commitment are large parts of the project.

What was the longest craft or art project you have done?

Is there one that you've always dreamed about but stopped short because of time?

Think of a way to get a small start. Learn the first step. Watch the Youtube video. Gather your materials.

This was my first ever quilt, a true labor of love.

I saw the pattern and in my head knew immediately what I wanted it to look like, except for the fact that I didn't know how to quilt or barely even sew.

It took months to learn how to paper piece blocks, then piece a quilt and it turned into a much larger project than I anticipated from my one little idea. The satisfaction was that much greater with all the work put in.

I asked my mom, mother in law, grandmas, and Godmother for words that represent a Christian woman and those became the border.

An extra special touch to be wrapped in those ideas!

you are
CREATIVE

Chapter Twenty

I am Creative

You might be thinking, *This would have been a great place to start* – and you're not wrong. Hopefully throughout the preceding pages you've gotten some inspiration and ideas of how you can use your own gifts.

Creativity to me is almost a double-edged sword. The best of changing or making something that's never been done before, balanced with the vulnerability that comes from wondering whether others will approve the work. This held me back (and to some degree still does).

I started a blog in 2012 while still in college for my education degree. I knew I had resources and lessons that other teachers, parents, and homeschool families could use in their classrooms. But it was easy to hide behind a screen; it was easy to fall into the "I don't have experience, so I can't contribute" trap.

I loved learning the technology, the platforms, the behind the scenes. I loved creating useful rigorous resources to help students learn tough material. I loved sharing classroom transformations, whether it be a cave, an operating room, or a Mario Party challenge.

The facts don't lie. Millions of people have since visited, left comments, and downloaded resources for their classrooms. These resources have impacted an innumerable number of students worldwide, and I still hear, *Who are you to do this? What value could they possibly find?*

Yes, sometimes **creativity is the ultimate form of vulnerability**. We choose to share our creativity *with* people but it's not the same as creating *for* them.

When you realize you're the only one standing in your way, the path clears up pretty quick.

God gave me a mind that can generate new ideas. I can bring inspiration, light, and smiles to others. Hiding it, or keeping it locked away in fear, isn't in His plans. This distinctly reminds me of Samuel thinking Eli was calling him in the night; finally he answers,

"Here I am; you called me" (1 Samuel 3:8).

Chances are if you picked up this book you have a creative mind too. One sometimes plagued with doubts, insecurity, and fear, and yet still you create. You take the chance, the risk, that your work will be appreciated or make a difference. It's not a small step, and in its own nature you honor the gift you were given.

When we change "Who am I to do this?" to "Here I am," we're standing firm and showing our bright light to others.

God, help me not to hide my gifts.

Take away all doubt and fear of rejection so I can **let my creativity shine** to bring light, smiles, and joy to those around me.

Thank you for giving me a mind open to enriching lives and gaining fulfillment through creating. Show me how to support others in their creative pursuits.

AMEN.

What is one negative belief you have about things you make? How can you reframe it in a positive, motivating way?

How would you describe a creative outlet you have? What makes it fulfilling?

Do you use your creative skills with others? How can you facilitate new ideas with another person or group?

Nothing says being creative and vulnerable like painting your garage door with chalkboard paint. We live on a busy road and I thought I could add jokes, messages or even verses for passersby to see.

Again I heard, "What if they think it's stupid?" "I've never seen it done before." "Who even cares?" and I still thought about the smile it could bring, the laugh over a shared joke or the backdrop for a photo and it was decided!

A quite literal spur of the moment idea turned into a changing fun display for our family! I still grin pushing the garage door button watching it unfold.

How could you use your creativity if there wasn't anyone (even yourself) stopping you?

you are
HOPEFUL

Chapter Twenty-One

I Am Hopeful

For a person who really holds tight to control, losing it feels pretty hopeless. I have a tendency to get stuck in the emotion, the moment, and not realize the bigger picture or even take a step back.

My marriage is in no way, shape or form what I thought it would be. Maybe it was the rose-colored glasses or the naivety that brought us together, and to some degree that's what made things stick. The commitment has not wavered but it's certainly not what I envisioned the day we said "I do." Wouldn't every day be sunshine and rainbows, with nary a disagreement or dispute?!

Learning as you go feels like keeping your head above water when you add in kids, parenting, and figuring out how to merge your lives together you steadily sink.

Communication wasn't sparse, but maybe the right kind of communication was. Once I texted my husband, *How can I pray for you this week?* I received, *Why are you asking me this?* – not in a curious way but an "I don't have time for this" way. We didn't have the foundation to build further and deeper conversations. We had many disagreements we didn't work through civilly. Nights we slept apart when the anger was still too close.

I always found myself praying, "What can I do to make this work? How can I change to be the wife I'm called to be? Change and soften my heart to truly hear and listen."

Over time and iwth lots of work together, one of my biggest revelations was, **If I win, we lose**. If I have to prove and get him to change his mind to my way, I'm not listening and I'm negating his viewpoint as my partner, which erodes our marriage. We are a team, and there is no room for one person to "win."

There is no one-size-fits-all-rule. Every relationship is different. Our relationship grows deeper and stronger, little by little our foundation strengthens and we do find and amass tools and strategies that work for us. In all of those in-between moments of doubt, anger, and indecision, there was hope. Hope in our commitment and hope in what was to come. Hope that it wouldn't always look this way.

> Faith in what we know and hope in the future. Hope that as an anchor (Hebrews 6:19) keeps us firm in the knowledge that heaven is our home.

While marriage may be an earthly institution, hope gives us positive momentum. Hope is the Holy Spirit, who keeps your heart set on the right path, comforting and guiding us on our way.

God, help me to keep You as my hope in this life.

When doubts, worry, or losing control threaten to move me, **remind me of my strong anchor of hope**.

Show me to keep hope in both good and troubling times, knowing our future with You.

AMEN.

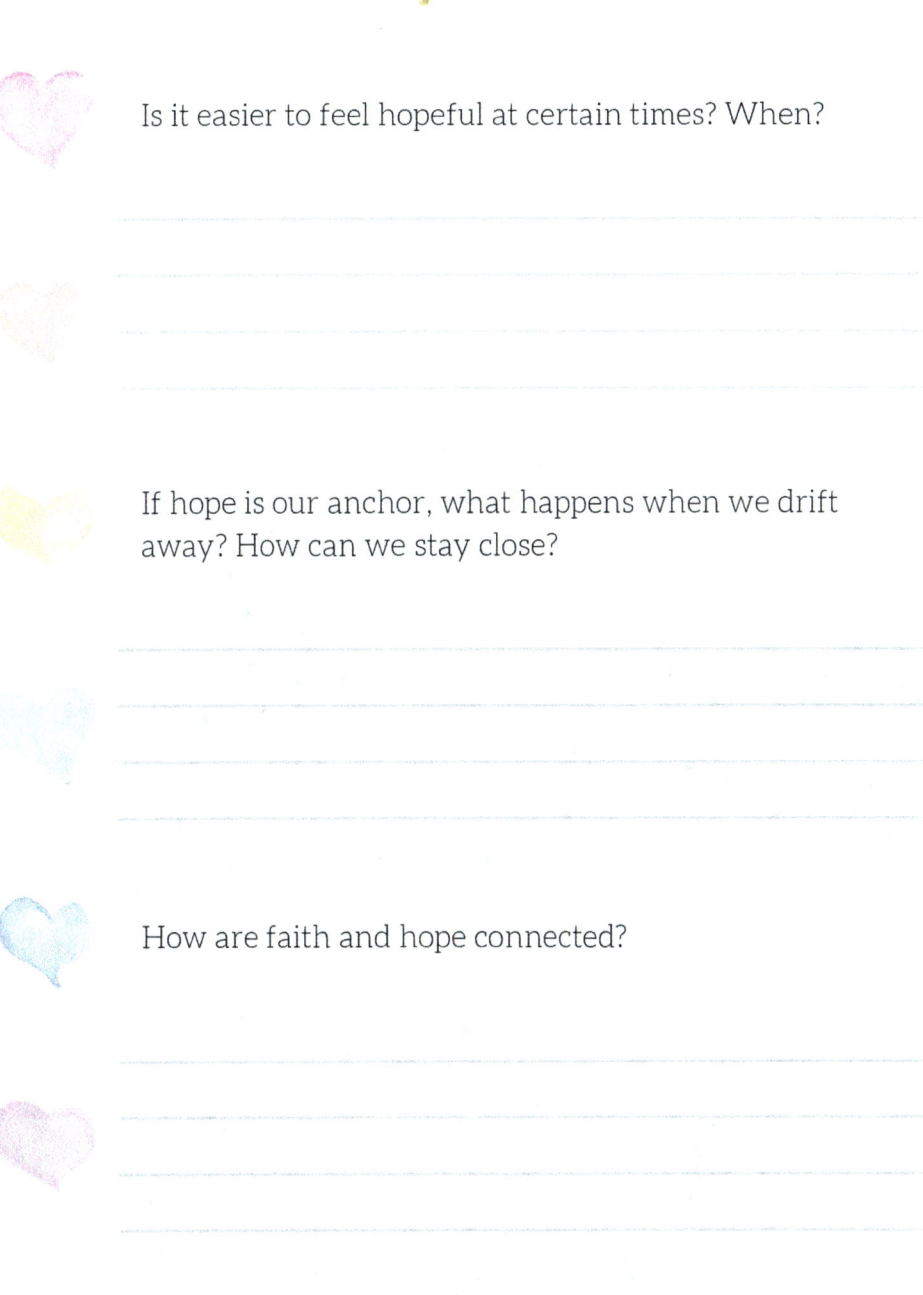

Is it easier to feel hopeful at certain times? When?

If hope is our anchor, what happens when we drift away? How can we stay close?

How are faith and hope connected?

I'm reminded of the MercyMe *Even If* song lyrics:

"I know the sorrow, I know the hurt
Would all go away if You'd just say the word
But even if You don't
My hope is You alone
It is well with my soul."

In times that feel that hopeless or that hope is far away our hope is in our Savior. Find this print in the *Templates* section. You can print and watercolor, use as a card, or reach out to someone!

Hope

anchors

the soul

you are
POSITIVE

Chapter Twenty-Two

I Am Positive

I have a confession to make: I'm a morning person. Through and through, up and at 'em, no caffeine needed. My mind is the freshest, cycling through ideas and planning out my day. Even in high school I would voluntarily put myself to bed early, feeling like my body needed rest.

At certain points in my life I'd try to fight it. Certainly sleeping in would be great, but my body would never cooperate. Staying up until midnight on New Year's—a thing of the past. The new year would be there when I woke up too.

As I've aged, I've realized that working by my natural rhythm makes way more sense. Lots of sleep, going to bed early, waking up and starting the day with attacking what I need to be at my best for, feels the best for me. That combination fuels me and gives me the best head start to my day. It helps keep me positive.

Setting yourself up for success is a huge way to stay positive, so when the trouble starts just like a small crack it doesn't break down your whole building.

The very first meal I cooked as a wife in our first apartment, two states away from home, ended in tons of smoke and a near fire alarm for the building on the day we moved in. My mother-in-law packed us a DIY pizza kit to take along for an easy meal when we arrived. We made the pizzas, heated the oven, but as I went to put them in they slid off the pan and straight into the oven itself.

It had already been a long day of driving, unloading, and unpacking, and that could easily have brought me down. I remember laughing it off because it truly was such a cliché that the first meal nearly ended in flames. I have no idea what we did end up eating, but I'm glad my outlook didn't erode the evening.

Even with rain (small and large events that threaten to cause doom and gloom) we hear in Genesis 9:16,

> "Whenever the rainbow appears in the clouds, I will see it and remember the everlasting covenant between God and all living creatures of every kind on the earth."

Our positive outlook can keep any situation from getting worse. **It shines a light reminding us where our true help comes from.** Sometimes we might see a brilliant rainbow and recognize the sign. Other times it may be the birds playing in a puddle, the funny line from a movie that becomes an inside joke, or just a friend's smile that conveys understanding.

God, keep a positive spirit in me, especially during hard, difficult or tough times.

Show me how to see the good, show the good and reflect the good for others.

Help me to see how You work all things out for those that love You just like You promised.

AMEN.

Reflect on some things you do to "set yourself up for success and positivity" List them here. Where else could you keep this important list?

What's the easiest way you can be a positive light to others?

In what are some future situations you might encounter, that a positive outlook may be helpful?

As my main career has been in education I like finding ways to uplift educators who spend so much time pouring into our kids.

Whether it be a light up goody box or maybe a capsule machine with chocolate and Bible verses, finding ways to bring a light to those serving others is always a good idea.

Positive Post its or fun notes are another small way to make a big difference. *Find two positive notes in the Templates section*

Who are some people who serve you and your family what could you do for them?

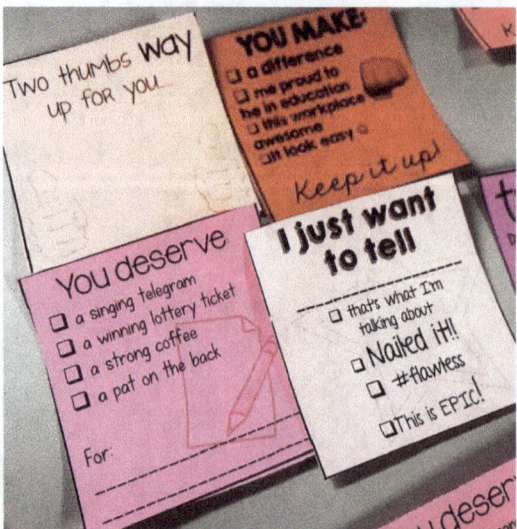

you are
PRESENT

Chapter Twenty-Three

I Am Present

I'm a high-strung person, so worrying and planning are second nature to me. I live for all the "possibilities" that could happen and have a plan for each of them. On the outside this may look seamless because you pivot so quickly, but mentally it takes up a huge amount of space.

Society puts so much pressure on people, especially women, to "soak up the moment." Make sure to enjoy every moment as it "goes too fast." I almost feel guilty letting anything slip through the cracks because it all adds up to some unattainable goal as a wife and mother. I even feel like I'm pretty good at this, and I still fail.

When we put together our last puzzle as a family and got to the home stretch with 50 or so pieces left, we each said, "Family puzzle" as we put a piece in. You could hear the tiny echoes as we all worked together toward our goal. The last piece we all had our fingers on and maneuvered together. In my "mind movie" our words and actions seared that memory as a moment of togetherness just like so many kitchen dance parties, growth chart markings, and daily singalongs that make our family "us."

On one of my birthday trips, we went snow tubing with my parents and our kids. We held hands and forged a chain of interconnected circle tubes and we flew down the hill blasted with mist. I remember thinking to myself, "I want to remember this." I want to remember the smiles on our faces, the wind in our hair, the utter delight of the experience together.

When I find myself focusing too much on past choices or worried about the future, two things really help me. **You can't be anxious and grateful at the same time**; it doesn't compute physiologically. So I just reframe my thinking to *I'm grateful for my job* if I'm worried about a presentation. *I'm so thankful for my children* when I'm anxious about a situation in school. It keeps me focused and helps me feel more present with what's happening externally. I'm not sure where I came upon this affirmation or if I made it up, but **I am right where I'm meant to be**. It sums up Jeremiah 29:11:

> "For I know the plans I have for you,' declares the Lord, 'plans to prosper you and not to harm you, plans to give you hope and a future."

God doesn't make mistakes, and if I'm still keeping him at the forefront, I'm on the right path. It gives so much freedom. There are no wrong moves—I'm doing the best I can with God's help, and that brings peace.

God, show me to stay focused on You right now and always.

Instead of worrying about the past, or being anxious for the future - **keep my mind in the present.**

Help me to see that I am right where I am meant to be through prayer with You.

AMEN.

Do you feel you are "right where you are meant to be"?
If not, how can you get closer?

What are one or two memories you can recall truly
being present for? How have they impacted you?

Being present can be actively listening to others (not
thinking about how it relates to you, waiting for them
to finish so you can speak) - how can you practice this
in your life?

Ernst Memories
2022

One way to capture gratefulness and to stay present is a memory book.

With no photos it serves as a family journal of sorts.

We record funny events, big moments, little treasures to remember.

A regular old journal works just as well!

What's great is that we can look back not just as pictures but stories from those times from years to come.

You can write in by yourself, leave on the table for anyone to add to, or even make it part of a weekly family meal, "does anyone have any additions for our book?"

If your kids are anything like mine, they LOVE looking back at pictures from years ago and I rarely print and make photo books. This is a tangible way to keep the memories.

TIP: I love **My Social Book** to print off my Facebook every year - it keeps comments, and QR codes for videos.

Many people like Chatbooks as well!

I am right where I am meant to be

you are
CURIOUS

Chapter Twenty-Four

I Am Curious

I would say I'm a naturally curious person. I love learning, taking in new information and finding the "why" behind how things work. I'm a really great replicator. I can see something, research how to do it, gather the materials and give it a go. Even just knowledge was something to be acquired. I would always frequent the library until the internet became an easier tool. Once I have a topic or idea I have to know everything. I soak it all up like a sponge. Organizing information, saving it for later or integrating it right away.

Curiousity doesn't always feel easy or helpful, though. Curiousity should maybe be defined as the pursuit of knowledge regardless of whether you realize the impact.

Curiosity led me to find out that I had a sister. Rummaging through a cabinet where our school pictures were kept, I found clipped newspaper pictures of a smiling blond girl at various ages. It wasn't anyone that I knew, so I was curious why we had them. My mom explained that the pictures were my sister and that my parents gave her up for adoption when they were younger. The family must have known we would be watching out and put pictures in the newspaper every year for her birthday.

That was one of the big awakenings where you realize your parents had lives before you and have roles that you don't see. You only see the part of them that starts after they had a child.

The thing about being curious—**you really don't know what you'll find**. Sometimes it's life altering (another sibling?!), sometimes it makes life easier (a fun new recipe!): either way, you'll always know more than you did before. You can process and decide where the information fits and how to move forward.

Not many people can say they met their sister in person at her wedding. Curiousity builds resilience as you learn how to integrate information more readily. Curiousity about beliefs led me to dig deep in the Bible, to find resources or people to answer my questions. To reflect on the Word and how it applies to my life. In Ecclesiastes 1:8 we hear,

"All things are wearisome, more than one can say. The eye never has enough of seeing, nor the ear its fill of hearing."

As we always know there could be more, staying curious— especially in the Word—keeps us grounded as we do learn new things and live in an ever-changing world.

God, help me to **stay curious** in all aspects of life.

Use my curiousity and learning to grow closer to You. When I learn new things, show me how they work together for Your good.

Show me how to keep growing and learning, molding me into the person You know I can be.

AMEN.

What topics have you always been drawn toward or want to learn more about?

_____

_____

_____

Is there a Bible topic, book, or story that was intriguing to you when you were younger? What about now?

_____

_____

_____

What do you do when you learn new information that doesn't fit with what know or believe?

_____

_____

_____

Curious might lead you to trying out new things and seeing if they work. During 2020, we really missed our family and friends that we weren't able to see in person. We made some yard signs (home supply stores) and with the help of a Cricut were able to deliver all around our area.

The idea was that the recipient would then pass on the sign to another family. **#covidkindnessyardsigns**

Getting out of the house, being "close" to others and spreading smiles made it all worth it!

Where will your curiousity take you? What new idea just waits to be uncovered?

Curiousity is the wick in the candle of learning

WILLIAM ARTHUR WARD

you are
PURPOSEFUL

Chapter Twenty-Five

I am Purposeful

We can think about all our gifts—how to use them, making the most of what we've been given. Sometimes that feels like a pressure cooker! Living each day to the fullest, helping all we can, keeping in control of our emotions every minute. Whew!

I found comfort in this Verse of Day I heard on the radio,

> "God has a purpose and plan for each of our lives. The greatest thing we can do is to find that purpose and live it out. We can trust His purpose for us because it is based on His wisdom and love. **As long as we seek His will, we're not going to do anything that can ultimately mess up his purpose for us.** Yes, we may at times stray from the perfect channel He wants us to travel, but we never get totally out of the main channel. As long as we do not abandon Him, and remember He will never forsake us, He will use us for His purposes." ("Verse of the Day: Psalm 138:8")

Something that lets some steam out of the pressure cooker is knowing that if I keep Him at the front, I can't mess it up. Even if I stray, I'm not alone and I keep going. It's ok if I don't have some magic plan and everything figured out. I have everything I need to keep going, and I know where to turn to for advice, comfort or help.

My life may feel open, but I can be content and at peace in my desire to control by realizing it's not up to me.

As you've been reading, some chapters may really resonate with you and others not as much. We each have our own multicolored unique set of gifts, our own "white light" we cast into the world—shining for others, lighting the path, following our purpose.

To close I want to leave you with one of the most reassuring Bible passages and one that encompasses so many of the gifts dicsussed. I slowly grew to love Psalm 23 as so many of my family members treasured the words. Bask in the comfort and solace on the next couple pages.

Write in your unique gifts on the rainbow outbursts below.
The ones that float right to the top, spilling out of you! What makes up your White Light?!

my
WHITE LIGHT.

The Lord is my shepherd; I shall not want.

He maketh me to lie down in green pastures: He leadeth me beside the still waters.

He restoreth my soul: He leadeth me in the paths of righteousness for His name's sake.

Yea, though I walk through the valley of the shadow of death, I will fear no evil: for Thou art with me; Thy rod and Thy staff they comfort me.

Thou preparest a table before me in the presence of mine enemies: Thou anointest my head with oil; my cup runneth over.

Surely goodness and mercy shall follow me all the days of my life: and I will dwell in the house of the Lord for ever.

I am
perserving

I am not
alone.

I am
traditional

I am
unifying

I am
worthy

I am
productive

I am
positive

I am
joyful

Break out the sparkly pens, the special pens, your favorite fine liners and color in the words on the next two pages that resonate with you. Take a moment as you fill it in considering how that gift is represented in your life.

lighthearted

persevering KNOWN

joyful

HOPEFUL strong

POSITIVE

LOVED

MERRY

FORGIVING

KIND observant

worthy

content

HELPFUL

PRESENT

NOT ALONE

unifying

traditional CA

GRATEFUL LM

PURPOSEFUL

restful curious

CREATIVE

TEMPLATES

let your light shine

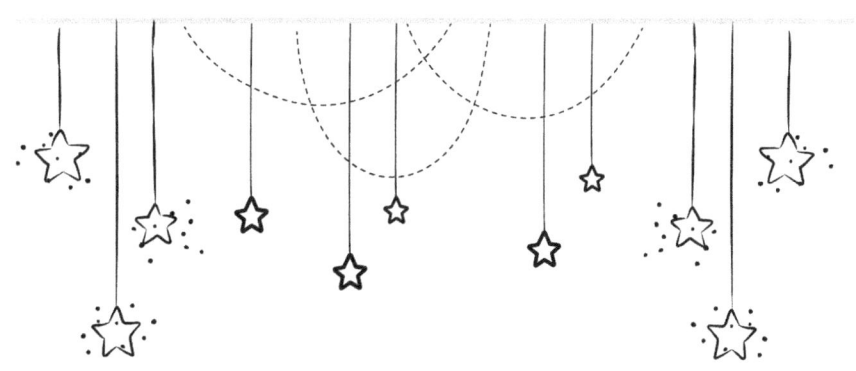

your sparkle has not
gone unnoticed

BECAUSE
I knew you
I HAVE
BEEN CHANGED
for good

WHEN I'M SINGING MY KIDS TO SLEEP....

I HAVE BEEN *blessed*

WHEN I FEEL YOU HOLDING ME...

My hope is you

NOW

it is well with my soul

You deserve:
- ☐ a singing telegram
- ☐ a winning lottery ticket
- ☐ a strong coffee
- ☐ a pat on the back

For:
_____
_____

You deserve:
- ☐ a singing telegram
- ☐ a winning lottery ticket
- ☐ a strong coffee
- ☐ a pat on the back

For:
_____
_____

You deserve:
- ☐ a singing telegram
- ☐ a winning lottery ticket
- ☐ a strong coffee
- ☐ a pat on the back

For:
_____
_____

You deserve:
- ☐ a singing telegram
- ☐ a winning lottery ticket
- ☐ a strong coffee
- ☐ a pat on the back

For:
_____
_____

You deserve:
- ☐ a singing telegram
- ☐ a winning lottery ticket
- ☐ a strong coffee
- ☐ a pat on the back

For:
_____
_____

You deserve:
- ☐ a singing telegram
- ☐ a winning lottery ticket
- ☐ a strong coffee
- ☐ a pat on the back

For:
_____
_____

I just want to tell
_____
☐ that's what I'm talking about
☐ Nailed it!!
☐ #flawless
☐ This is EPIC!

I just want to tell
_____
☐ that's what I'm talking about
☐ Nailed it!!
☐ #flawless
☐ This is EPIC!

I just want to tell
_____
☐ that's what I'm talking about
☐ Nailed it!!
☐ #flawless
☐ This is EPIC!

I just want to tell
_____
☐ that's what I'm talking about
☐ Nailed it!!
☐ #flawless
☐ This is EPIC!

I just want to tell
_____
☐ that's what I'm talking about
☐ Nailed it!!
☐ #flawless
☐ This is EPIC!

I just want to tell
_____
☐ that's what I'm talking about
☐ Nailed it!!
☐ #flawless
☐ This is EPIC!

DOODLE BOOKMARKS

Download 24 bookmarks ready for you to unleash your creative side and share with friends and family!

About Author

Amber is a wife and mom to two amazing boys. Amber has worked in the education field for over 10 years and has been blogging at SSSTeaching, Sparkles, Smiles, and Successful Students, since 2012. Her *sparkly* side led her to combine passions and publish her first book, <u>White Light</u>, to see how she could help others connect to their purpose creatively in a chaotic world. You can find Amber hosting parties, playing games with the family, or taking quiet walks, probably dreaming up ways to add some sparkle or color to someone's life.

Join our book community and use **#mywhitelight** to share about your journey and ideas!

Acknowledgments

A most heartfelt thank you to my husband, who never waivered in his support—from encouraging me when the book was just an idea, to a sounding board then finally to an editor when it all came together. I am a better version of myself and continue to grow with you by my side.

Many thanks to Logan and Sam, my beautiful boys; you are a continued source of inspiration. I may grow in motherhood every day, but your laughs, smiles, and "kiss your brain" moments always have me thinking, *How did God know exactly who I need?* I try to lock away every special memory, joke or hug knowing all too soon this time will be gone. I watch astounded as I see your personalities and your own gifts develop as well—what a lucky world that has you both in it.

Thank you to Micah Ernst whose revisions made sure this book was in line with God's Word. Micah and continues to serve as an example of living his purpose daily. Thank you for treating these words carefully knowing how much it meant to me.

Thank you to Haylee Anderson, the copywriting extraordinaire. I've never had to trust really personal writing with anyone else before and you took it in stride. Your communication made me feel at ease and made the project come together seamlessly.

Finally thank you, dear reader. It might not be a traditional connection, but you took a chance and read this book—and I'm grateful.

References

Hepworth, Sally. *The Mother-in-Law*. St. Martin's Press, 2019.

Ingrid Fetell Lee. *Joyful : The Surprising Power of Ordinary Things to Create Extraordinary Happiness*. London, Rider Books, 2020.

"Verse of the Day: Psalm 138:8." *Www.verseoftheday.com*, Heartlight Inc, 29 June 2022, www.verseoftheday.com/en/06292022/. Accessed 29 June 2022.

Zondervan. *NIV Holy Bible*. 2012.

www.ingramcontent.com/pod-product-compliance
Lightning Source LLC
Chambersburg PA
CBHW060527150626
46553CB00023B/620